CYBERSECURITY L̶ ̶ ̶ ̶ FOR SENIORS

Mastering Cybersecurity in the Age of AI and Quantum Computing: A Comprehensive Guide to Safeguarding Against Advanced Threats, IoT Vulnerabilities

Nathaniel Nicholas

Copyright

Contents

Description

Unlock the keys of quantifying cybersecurity risk and safeguarding your company from digital threats. This is a Data-Driven Guide to Measuring, Monitoring, and Mitigating Digital Threats. This comprehensive book is for professionals who desire practical, results-oriented approaches to boost their security posture in today's fast-expanding cyber ecosystem. This book explores critical cybersecurity metrics like Mean Time to Detect (MTTD) and Annualized Loss Expectancy (ALE) through easy-to-follow explanations and real-world examples, enabling you to analyse and convey risk impact accurately.

This book covers key arears about Cyber security like:

Essential frameworks like NIST, ISO 27001, and CIS Controls help link risk measurement with industry requirements.

- How to estimate and decrease risk using quantitative risk analysis, including Monte Carlo simulations and Bayesian inference.

- Step-by-step templates for continuous monitoring, data collection, and reporting, making it easy to implement effective cybersecurity procedures immediately.

And lots more...

Written by a specialist in cyber risk management, this book offers a refreshing, educative, and engaging insight. It breaks down complex topics using understandable language and hands-on techniques. Whether you're a cybersecurity specialist, IT manager, or company leader, this book is a critical resource to help you stay one step ahead of cyber dangers.

With CYBERSECURITY LAWS FOR SENIORS, you won't just react to security threats—you'll be prepared to foresee, measure, and manage them. Don't wait until the following incident—take action today to secure a safer digital future for your firm.

Introduction

When I started researching cybersecurity, the concept of "risk" seemed daunting. The dilemma of evaluating something as complicated and dynamic as cybersecurity risk persisted, particularly in today's fast-changing digital landscape. Today, every firm, regardless of size or industry, faces cybersecurity dangers, ranging from data breaches and phishing scams to insider threats and ransomware assaults. And let's face it: the stakes are tremendous. A single cyber event can disrupt operations, degrade a brand, and cause millions of dollars in losses. In many ways, cybersecurity risk has become an integral component of modern company strategy. Imagine a world where businesses kept their doors open, hoping for the best—unthinkable, right? However, without effective cybersecurity risk measurement, that is precisely what we do in the digital world.

Because these risks affect an organization's data, operations, and reputation, effectively monitoring and controlling them is critical to its long-term viability and success. One of the most severe consequences of cybersecurity risk is financial loss. The average data breach now costs firms millions of dollars in direct expenses, including investigation, response, legal fees, and, probably most importantly, a loss of customer trust. Beyond financial costs, these accidents harm an organization's reputation, hinder business continuity, and frequently result in legal ramifications.

In other words, cyber risk is complex, influencing everything from a company's profitability to its long-term survival. However, not all cybersecurity dangers are apparent or easily quantifiable. They differ from more concrete hazards, such as physical security threats or asset losses.

In cybersecurity, risks are frequently invisible and continuously developing, making standard risk measurement approaches appear obsolete. So, how do we move forward? How can we identify and quantify cybersecurity threats in an understandable and actionable way?

The Challenge of Quantifying Risk: Why Traditional Methods Fail

Let's face it: it's challenging to estimate cybersecurity risk. For decades, corporations have used traditional risk assessment methods—financial models, risk matrices, and qualitative analysis—to assess everything from investment risks to environmental threats. However, cybersecurity risk is inherently complex. Based on past data, traditional models frequently presume that risk is static or quantifiable. However, this static approach is ineffective in cybersecurity, where new threats might appear at any time. Traditional risk models are limited in reacting to dynamic, developing risks.

For example, suppose you evaluate your risk level and determine your organization's vulnerability to ransomware. A few weeks later, a new form of ransomware emerges, avoiding your detection techniques. Your entire risk assessment is outdated, making you vulnerable to previously unknown attack methods. This unpredictability is characteristic of cyber dangers, necessitating a more adaptable, responsive approach to risk assessment.

Another issue with old methods is that they frequently rely on subjective assessments. In a risk matrix, for example, we could label a hazard as "high," "medium," or "low." But what do these terms mean? One person's "high" may be another's "medium." A lack of accuracy in cybersecurity can lead to misconceptions, inconsistent decision-making, and potentially costly mistakes.

However, the most significant disadvantage is that traditional methodologies in cybersecurity lack a data-driven base. Without accurate data to back up our assessments, we are left with assumptions. This is when measurable objectives and data collecting come into play.

This book will expose you to a lot of secrets that have been hidden from you. It's the last ever book you would ever need on cybersecurity.

Get a copy for yourself....

Chapter 1

Introduction to Cybersecurity Risk Measurement

Consider a modest goal, such as eliminating phishing attacks. We could say, "We want to reduce phishing attacks," but it is ambiguous. A better attainable target would be: "We aim to reduce phishing attack incidents by 20% over the next 12 months through employee training and improved filtering technologies." That's a target we can track and evaluate. If the quantity of phishing attacks does not decrease, we know that something in our strategy needs to change. Data is the foundation of measurable goals, laying the groundwork for our risk assessments. Without data, our risk evaluations are simply educated assumptions. Fortunately, in the digital era, we have access to more data than ever, including threat intelligence platforms, intrusion detection systems, user activity logs, and more. The problem is to filter through this data to identify meaningful insights. Data enables us to move from "We think this is a problem" to "Here's the evidence of our risk exposure, and here's how it's changing over time." It allows us to quantitatively assess cybersecurity risks using solid evidence rather than intuition or conjecture. We can track event frequency, identify system weaknesses, and quantify specific risks' financial impact with the correct data.

Introduction to Key Measurement Concepts and Terminology.

First, let's define some essential words. These will serve as our guideposts as we continue reading the book.

Risk is the likelihood of an adverse event occurring and its potential consequences. In cybersecurity, risk typically refers to threats (such as malware or phishing) that exploit vulnerabilities (such as software defects) to compromise valuable assets (such as sensitive data).

Threats are defined as anything that has the potential to harm an organization. This involves external actors such as hackers, including natural disasters, unintentional human blunders, and internal misconduct.

Vulnerabilities are "weak spots" in our systems that attackers can exploit. They could be technological, like out-of-date software, or human, such as insufficient employee training.

Impact: This is the result of a risk materializing. Impacts can be financial, operational, or reputational. Quantifying impact is crucial because it allows us to prioritize risks based on their potential damage.

Likelihood is the probability of a risk event occurring. Determining likelihood is difficult in cybersecurity because it frequently requires a combination of historical data, threat intelligence, and expert judgment.

Residual risk refers to the danger that persists after security measures have been implemented. It is critical to remember that no security solution completely removes risk; there will always be some residual risk that we must tolerate.

These concepts may appear simple, but they are essential for developing a solid risk measurement strategy. When we discuss cybersecurity risk in this book, we'll use these terms—risk, threat, vulnerability, impact, likelihood, and residual risk—so understanding them is essential.

Cybersecurity Risk and Its Impact on Modern Organizations

Cybersecurity risk is more than just a buzzword; it is a reality that modern businesses must deal with daily. It impacts all company levels, from financial performance to day-to-day operations and long-term brand reputation. To appreciate the scale and stakes of cybersecurity risk, consider these real-world occurrences and how they affected businesses of various sizes and industries.

Example 1: Target's Data Breach: Financial Impact and Customer Trust. During the holiday shopping season in 2013, Target, one of the significant retail firms in the United States, experienced a massive data breach. Over 40 million consumers' credit card and personal information were stolen after hackers accessed its networks.

The intrusion was tracked back to network credentials obtained from a third-party vendor, a heating and air conditioning business. Using this seemingly trivial weakness, attackers accessed Target's payment systems.

The financial toll was tremendous. Target spent over $200 million on customer compensation, legal fees, and system changes to improve its cybersecurity. Beyond the economic implications, the intrusion shattered customer trust. Retail relies greatly on consumer trust, and for months after the incident, Target suffered from falling customer satisfaction levels. The incident was a solid warning for businesses worldwide: cybersecurity is more than simply an IT issue; it is a brand and financial imperative.

In response, Target made significant modifications to its cybersecurity processes. They changed vendor management practices, installed two-factor authentication, and set up a specialized cyber response team. The lessons learned from that breach continue to impact Target's policy today.

They've gone proactive, including cybersecurity in their operating plans and stressing vendor security. This transformation demonstrates how a single occurrence may change corporate practices and priorities at all levels.

Example 2: Small Business Ransomware Attack, Operational Halt

Large firms such as Target are not the only ones in danger. Smaller enterprises, which frequently lack the cybersecurity expenditures of industry titans, are popular targets for cybercriminals. Consider a real-world example with a tiny accounting firm in the Midwest. They were targeted by a ransomware attack just before tax season, peak business time.

Hackers took over the firm's networks, encrypting all client files and demanding a large payment. With limited resources and no real-time backups, the firm had to make a critical decision: pay the ransom or risk losing all of its clients' data. They chose to pay, but not without facing severe penalties. Beyond the financial loss caused by the ransom, the firm endured operational interruption for nearly two weeks, frustrating clients and incurring service delays.

The operational impact of cyber events is frequently neglected, but it was likely the most severe in this case. Clients went for competitors, questioning the firm's dependability and security. Since then, the company has invested in solid backup systems, multilayered security processes, and client communication strategies during catastrophes. This little business tale demonstrates that, even without the massive resources of a large corporation, cybersecurity must be a critical component of operations.

Example 3: The Reputational Impact of Uber's Data Breach Cover-Up

Not all cybersecurity impacts are evident in financial accounts; reputational damage is frequently longer-lasting and more difficult to assess. In 2016, Uber suffered a massive data breach, exposing the personal information of over 57 million users and drivers. However, Uber paid the hackers $100,000 rather than revealing the breach to keep the event quiet.

The cover-up was eventually exposed a year later, causing public indignation and undermining trust. The cash impact in this situation was less than it was for Target, but the reputational damage was enormous. Trust is critical for any organization that deals with personal data, and Uber's handling of the incident sparked widespread criticism. Users, authorities, and the general public questioned Uber's honesty, resulting in increased scrutiny and a tarnished brand reputation that Uber spent years attempting to recover.

Following the incident, Uber overhauled its data security policies, adopting a more transparent and security-conscious approach. The corporation developed more demanding incident response practices, such as prompt disclosure and cooperation with regulators. This shift towards transparency demonstrates how a cybersecurity catastrophe may radically change an organization's attitude to ethical responsibility, privacy, and brand management.

Chapter 2

How Cybersecurity Risk Shapes Organizational Policies and Business Decisions

Cybersecurity isn't just about responding to incidents; it's about proactively crafting policy and business decisions to prevent them. Every high-profile data breach, ransomware attack, or insider threat is a lesson, leading firms to reassess their strategies. Here's how cybersecurity risk has altered business policy and decision-making across sectors.

Policy Evolution: Vendor and Third-Party Risk Management

Target's breach was a wake-up call for firms depending on third-party vendors. Today, many firms have established more robust third-party risk management policies, setting greater cybersecurity expectations for their vendors. Companies increasingly analyze the security posture of their vendors before signing contracts and impose rigorous access controls. This move highlights how cybersecurity concerns extend beyond a company's internal processes and into its commercial environment.

Investment in Cybersecurity Training and Awareness: Cybersecurity concerns have forced firms to treat cybersecurity as a company-wide responsibility. Employee training has become routine to prevent human error, a primary source of security accidents.

Phishing simulations, cybersecurity awareness workshops, and policy updates on secure device usage are just a few examples of training activities. The small accounting firm's lack of awareness and backup preparedness led to devastating downtime. Now, firms of all sizes spend training to develop a culture of alertness, understanding that every employee has a role in securing company data.

Shift Toward Data Transparency and Trust Building: For organizations like Uber, cybersecurity risk has inspired a shift toward greater transparency and trust-building. Organizations are now more likely to disclose problems swiftly, focused on limiting reputational harm by being honest with consumers and authorities.

This transition is critical, especially when privacy legislation like GDPR forces organizations to notify breaches within a set timeframe. Transparent rules reflect a commitment to data protection, fostering closer relationships with consumers and the public.

Strengthening Incident Response and Resilience: Incident response strategies have evolved substantially recently. Companies now focus on resilience—how quickly they can recover from a catastrophe and return to normal operations.

This resilience mindset is visible in large organizations that regularly test and modify their incident response plans, simulating attacks to prepare for worst-case scenarios. Effective response not only saves downtime but also reassures stakeholders that the company is capable of handling crises without substantial disruptions.

Rethinking Business Models and Digital Transformation:

Finally, cybersecurity risk is influencing company models and digital transformation activities. As firms increasingly rely on digital technologies and data-driven decision-making, they face new vulnerabilities. Business decisions today routinely involve cybersecurity professionals to examine risks connected with new technology, cloud storage, remote work, and more. Security has become critical in digital transformation, impacting how firms innovate and flourish.

Challenges in Quantifying Cybersecurity Risk

Many organizations still rely on old methodologies, such as risk matrices and qualitative assessments, which typically fall short when assessing cybersecurity risk. Cyber threats are dynamic, sophisticated, and constantly evolving—these features alone make it impossible to quantify cybersecurity risk using static models. Traditional methodologies are founded on historical data and defined probabilities, making them less adaptive to today's dynamically evolving cyber threat scene.

Let's explore these problems more deeply with a few instances, comparing classic and new ways and highlighting why a more adaptable, data-driven process is needed for assessing cyber risk in 2024.

1. Traditional Risk Matrices:

The Limitation of Static Measurements

Risk matrices are a standard technique for measuring risk across sectors. They plot the likelihood of an event happening against its potential impact, categorizing risks as low, medium, or high. This method is simple and straightforward, and on paper, it appears feasible. However, in cybersecurity, this paradigm soon displays its limits.

Consider a hospital utilizing a risk matrix to identify potential cyber hazards. Using past data, the hospital's cybersecurity team places "ransomware attack" in the "medium likelihood, high impact" category. However, during the past year, ransomware assaults in the healthcare industry have skyrocketed. Threat actors have evolved new, sophisticated strategies, and the chance of ransomware outbreaks has doubled throughout the industry. The difficulty with a static risk matrix is its inability to represent the changing nature of cyber threats. The hospital's judgment, based on old data, no longer represents current dangers. When the actual risk level increases, the matrix remains unchanged unless adjusted manually.

If upgrades are rare or missed, enterprises are left with a false sense of security. This hospital scenario demonstrates the need for adaptive tools that adjust to changing threat landscapes in real time.

Modern methods, such as dynamic risk scoring systems, overcome this issue. These systems use continuous threat intelligence feeds to give real-time risk assessments based on current data. Instead of static placements on a grid, dynamic scores reflect fluctuations in threat activity, enabling companies to always maintain an accurate awareness of risk levels.

2. The Problem of Subjectivity in Qualitative Analysis:

Traditional cybersecurity evaluations frequently rely on qualitative methods—risk rankings that depend on subjective judgments by analysts. Take the example of a medium-sized financial services organization assessing insider threats. Without precise data, the team might assess insider threats as "medium" risk based on a general view of the company's culture and trust in its personnel. This method introduces a layer of subjectivity that might obfuscate reality. In 2024, insider dangers have developed, with remote and hybrid employment becoming the norm. Employees now access company resources from personal devices, home networks, and public Wi-Fi.

This company's evaluation might substantially underestimate the potential harm without adaptive methods that measure insider threat risk based on real-world behavior patterns. To tackle this, many firms are turning to behavioral analytics technologies. These technologies quantify insider dangers by examining patterns like login timings, access frequency, and unexpected activity spikes. These solutions provide objective measurements that identify shifts in behavior, allowing security teams to detect insider hazards before they worsen. This transition from subjective analysis to data-backed insights transforms how firms perceive and handle insider threats, enabling a more exact understanding of internal risk.

3. Inflexibility of Compliance-Based Models:

Many firms rely significantly on compliance frameworks, such as NIST, ISO 27001, and CIS Controls, as their primary way of controlling cybersecurity risk. While compliance provides a good baseline, it's not a one-size-fits-all answer. Compliance frameworks are often prescriptive, requiring specified steps without always allowing for individual business risks. This rigidity might leave firms vulnerable to developing risks outside the compliance scope.

For instance, in 2021, Colonial Pipeline, a primary U.S. energy provider, faced a ransomware attack that affected petroleum supply across the East Coast.

The organization complies with necessary cybersecurity regulations, although the attack exploited vulnerabilities that typical compliance approaches didn't address. Colonial's compliance-based risk assessment hadn't prepared for the new ransomware threats targeting vital infrastructure. In response, the corporation paid millions in ransom, revealing how compliance alone couldn't safeguard against growing cyber risks.

Modern techniques increasingly emphasize adaptive risk frameworks that combine compliance with constant threat monitoring. Threat intelligence feeds, risk-based vulnerability management, and real-time data from SIEM (Security Information and Event Management) systems are examples of corporations expanding compliance frameworks and turning static standards into a more dynamic, flexible security posture.

4. Inadequate Handling of Unknown Threats – The Zero-Day Conundrum

Zero-day vulnerabilities are security defects in software or hardware that attackers exploit before the vendor publishes a fix. Traditional risk models struggle with zero days because they rely on previous data to predict probability and impact, whereas zero-day risks are, by nature, unknown until they are identified.

In 2024, fraudsters are increasingly targeting zero-day vulnerabilities. This trend illustrates the inadequacy of previous data in assessing danger from unknown hazards. Imagine a tech corporation employing a typical risk model to measure the threat of illegal access.

Their algorithm might imply a low risk based on previous data. Yet, the low-risk assessment is immediately obsolete if a zero-day vulnerability arises in a widely used software package.

Adaptive, data-driven strategies like predictive analytics are helping firms bridge this gap. Predictive models evaluate data trends to forecast future weaknesses, providing a forward-looking approach to risk assessment. While predictive analytics can't discover specific zero days, they offer insights into prospective risk areas, allowing security teams to spend resources preemptively.

5. Outdated Cost-Estimation Models for Cyber Incidents:

Traditional cost assessment approaches for cyber disasters frequently rely on static averages—X amount for each breached record or Y dollars in legal fees. However, these models can't reflect the subtle repercussions of a cyber attack, which vary depending on factors including industry, incident intensity, and the form of the leaked data.

A prominent illustration of this issue may be observed in the financial sector, where data breaches regularly generate regulatory fines that traditional models overlook. In 2022, a sizeable worldwide bank experienced a data breach that damaged its customers' financial information.

The conventional cost model overestimated the impact, failing to account for regulatory penalties, missed commercial prospects, and reputational loss. The actual cost exceeded predictions by approximately 50%.

Companies now utilize more detailed, incident-specific cost prediction algorithms to increase accuracy. These models account for direct and indirect expenses, including reputational damage and future business loss. By upgrading cost assessment methods, firms can obtain a realistic view of prospective losses and plan appropriately, making better-informed cybersecurity investments.

Defining Measurable Goals and Data's Role in Risk Assessment

One of the most significant shifts in cybersecurity is transitioning from reactive to proactive strategies. In my view, a substantial part of that progress is defining clear, quantifiable goals that specify what we're striving for and how we'll know if we're reaching the target. Regarding cybersecurity, "we want to reduce risk" isn't detailed enough. Instead, developing measurable goals transforms uncertain ideals into achievable aims, offering a blueprint for effective cybersecurity operations.

Let's examine quantifiable targets in several cybersecurity domains, how to collect data to measure progress, and some best practices for making the most of data-centric evaluations.

Examples of Measurable Cybersecurity Goals Across Key Areas

1. Reducing Phishing Attacks Through Employee Training

Instead of a broad aim to "reduce phishing incidents," a measurable goal would look like this: "Reduce phishing incidents by 25% over the next six months by implementing regular training and phishing simulations." This goal includes a target and a timeline, vital for measuring progress.

2. Improving Incident Response Time

Quick incident reaction is crucial in cybersecurity. For a measurable target, we would state, "Reduce average response time to detected threats from five hours to under two hours within the next quarter." By focusing on precise response times, firms can optimize operations, track improvement, and ultimately limit the effect of crises.

3. Enhancing Vulnerability Management Efficiency

In vulnerability management, a measurable target could be, "Increase patch deployment within 48 hours for all high-priority vulnerabilities, achieving 90% compliance over the next three months." This aim is concise and actionable and provides easy tracking of patch management success, which is critical for quickly eliminating security vulnerabilities.

4. Increasing Threat Detection Accuracy

A measurable goal for a company utilizing an Intrusion Detection System (IDS) would be to "Achieve a 10% reduction in false positives within the next six months by optimizing detection algorithms." This goal prioritizes data quality and boosts detection capabilities, lowering the load of false alarms on cybersecurity personnel.

5. Boosting Endpoint Security

A measurable target for firms focusing on endpoint security may be, "Ensure all company-issued devices have endpoint protection software installed and updated, with 95% compliance within the next month." This clear and measurable aim emphasizes the need to safeguard endpoints while workers operate from diverse places.

Chapter 3

Data Collection Methods, Tools, and Types of Data for Cybersecurity

Collecting the correct data is critical for assessing progress toward these goals. Data isn't simply numbers—the proof of what's working and what isn't. Here's an overview of effective data collection methods, tools, and data types to examine in a cybersecurity-focused risk assessment.

- Threat Intelligence Feeds:

Threat intelligence platforms combine data on known and developing threats from the Internet, the dark web, and other sources. Tools like Recorded Future, Anomali, or FireEye's Threat Intelligence can provide ongoing visibility into potential hazards, allowing teams to assess the number and nature of attacks targeting their industry.

For example, a financial institution might use a threat intelligence feed to notice increased phishing assaults intended at comparable firms, letting it alter its defenses proactively.

- SIEM (Security Information and Event Management) Systems:

SIEM systems, such as Splunk, IBM QRadar, and ArcSight, are the backbone of data collecting in cybersecurity. They collect and analyze log data from across an organization's network, helping detect unusual activities. For example, by setting up specific criteria within a SIEM solution, a corporation can monitor login attempts, data transfer patterns, or access to essential files, making it easier to notice potential insider threats or external attacks.

- User Behavior Analytics (UBA):

User activity Analytics systems like Exabeam and Varonis analyze individual user activity, producing baselines and identifying anomalies. UBA tools warn security professionals if an employee regularly logs in from one area but suddenly enters the network from an odd region. These technologies are particularly beneficial for tracking measurable goals connected to insider threats or unauthorized access, as they provide concrete data on deviations from typical behavior.

- Endpoint Detection and Response (EDR):

EDR systems like CrowdStrike Falcon, Carbon Black, and SentinelOne continuously monitor endpoint activities. They capture data about application activity, network connections, and device user interactions. Suppose the goal is to boost endpoint security compliance. In that case, EDR products allow teams to monitor device security status in real time, displaying which endpoints are secured, up to date, and compliant with security standards.

- Phishing Simulation Platforms:

Phishing simulation systems such as KnowBe4 and PhishMe send phony phishing emails to employees, tracking how many fall for the bait. This data directly informs training efficacy. For instance, if a measurable aim is to decrease phishing susceptibility, analyzing click rates from these simulations gives information into training impact, allowing organizations to identify where further effort might be needed.

- Vulnerability Scanning Tools:

Vulnerability scanners like Nessus, Qualys, and Rapid7 InsightVM continuously check for holes across an organization's infrastructure. By reviewing data on detected vulnerabilities, patch status, and criticality ratings, companies may track their vulnerability management goals, focusing resources on high-risk areas and limiting exposure to known threats.

Best Practices for Data-Driven Risk Assessments

For firms new to data-driven risk assessment, starting with best practices can set them on the right road. Here's how to optimize the impact of data in a cybersecurity risk assessment:

- Start with Clear Goals and Metrics

Measurable goals drive data gathering; therefore, specify goals before deploying data tools. Clarity helps determine which data to collect, whether the goal is to reduce phishing rates, limit incident response times, or improve endpoint security. Avoid imprecise targets; instead, focus on measures that provide actionable data, such as response times, patching speed, or employee training rates.

- Prioritize Data Quality Over Quantity:

Not all info is helpful. Collecting enormous amounts of data without filtering for relevance creates "noise" that obscures critical findings. Focus on obtaining high-quality, relevant data that corresponds with your aims. For instance, if the purpose is to increase detection accuracy, prioritize data that reflects actual threat patterns and user activity rather than relying on broad, general log data.

- Automate Data Collection and Analysis:

Manual data gathering can easily become overwhelming, especially in large enterprises. Automation solutions like SIEMs, EDRs, and UBA tools speed the data collection process, capturing insights in real-time and lowering the margin for human error. Automation also provides faster incident response by immediately alerting security staff when anomalous activity is discovered.

- Regularly Review and Adjust Goals Based on Data Insights:

Data collecting and goal-setting are iterative processes. As new risks emerge and systems evolve, businesses should periodically review acquired data and adjust goals accordingly. For example, if endpoint monitoring data suggests an increase in unlawful USB drive usage, a new target can focus on limiting such access. Adjusting goals keeps risk assessment relevant, adapting to current threat landscapes.

- Implement Visualization Tools for Better Insights:

Raw data is complex to interpret without good visualization. Dashboards and visualizations simplify complex data, making it easier for decision-makers to grasp cybersecurity concerns at a glance. Tools like Tableau or Power BI may assist in showing data trends, such as phishing susceptibility over time or the number of reported vulnerabilities each month, converting numbers into actionable insights.

- Encourage Cross-Department Collaboration:

Cybersecurity isn't only an IT issue. Data-driven insights are valuable across departments, from compliance to HR to operations. Regular cross-departmental meetings to examine data-driven risk assessments foster a collaborative approach to cybersecurity, developing a coherent culture that sees risk as a shared responsibility.

Chapter 4

How to Implement a Data-Centric Approach in a Small Business

Imagine a modest e-commerce business striving to improve its cybersecurity posture. The company's measurable goal is to reduce failed login attempts by 30% within six months to prevent account takeover attempts. Here's how a data-driven approach can look in action:

Goal Definition: The team creates a precise aim and schedule, concentrating on measurable decreases in failed login attempts.

Data Collection: They build a rudimentary SIEM tool that monitors login attempts, failed authentications, and times of access, automatically identifying problematic trends.

Analysis and Adjustment: The data reveals a rise in failed logins during specified hours, prompting the organization to deploy two-factor authentication for high-risk periods.

Monitoring Progress: As employees receive training and 2FA is installed, the SIEM tool tracks progress, providing a month-by-month drop in failed login attempts.

Review and Adaptation: After six months, the company analyzes its progress. Not only did failed attempts diminish, but customer support reported fewer account-related complaints. Seeing this accomplishment, the team sets new targets focusing on more significant security issues, utilizing the initial project as a paradigm for further data-centric improvements.

Data Measurement Concepts and Terminology

When it comes to analyzing cybersecurity risk, having a thorough grasp of key measurement concepts is vital. These phrases aren't simply technical jargon—they reflect meaningful measurements that drive our knowledge of where a company stands in terms of cybersecurity and what actions are needed. Here, we'll discuss some of the most critical concepts, breaking down each word with real-world events to make them more relevant.

1. Mean Time to Detect (MTTD)

Definition: MTTD estimates the average time it takes for an organization to notice a security event. This metric is crucial because the sooner we discover an occurrence, the faster we can respond, limiting potential damage.

Scenerio: Imagine a huge retail corporation that maintains sensitive client data, including credit card information. They have a security system in place, but it takes an average of 12 hours for the team to notice a potential threat, from the point of infiltration to the initial detection. During those 12 hours, a cybercriminal might access or change critical data, potentially causing substantial damage.

To improve MTTD, the organization might invest in more robust detection technologies, such as a Security Information and Event Management (SIEM) system with advanced analytics.

Suppose they can reduce MTTD from 12 hours to just 3. In that case, they drastically lessen the chance of data exfiltration, providing the team with a more significant opportunity to secure client information before a breach becomes catastrophic.

MTTD is especially crucial for areas where any delay in identifying a danger can imply considerable losses or regulatory concerns, such as finance or healthcare. In 2024, with more complex threats, the focus on decreasing MTTD will continue to expand across sectors.

2. Mean Time to Respond (MTTR)

Definition: MTTR measures the average time it takes for an organization to respond to a detected incident. A rapid response helps contain and remediate the issue, decreasing the possibility of harm to the organization.

Scenario: Let's suppose a healthcare provider with sensitive patient records. They undergo a phishing assault where an employee unintentionally clicks on a fraudulent link, giving attackers access to the system. Once the incident is recognized, the time on MTTR starts ticking.

In this example, if it takes the team another 8 hours to respond and mitigate the problem, attackers have adequate opportunity to access and breach patient records. By investing in automated response systems or employing tools like endpoint detection and response (EDR), the healthcare provider can seek to reduce MTTR to under an hour, ensuring that any detected danger is rapidly contained.

The goal with MTTR is always to reduce downtime and prevent further harm. In areas like healthcare and banking, where delays can lead to compliance breaches, a short MTTR is critical for operational resilience.

3. Risk Appetite

Definition: Risk appetite refers to the level of risk a company is ready to accept in pursuit of its objectives. Understanding risk appetite helps businesses identify which threats are tolerated and which require quick action in cybersecurity.

Scenario: Imagine a financial services corporation with a high-risk appetite for creative ventures, such as launching a new digital wallet function. While the organization recognizes the danger of cyber threats involved with rolling out a digital financial product, it deems the potential benefits worth the investment in additional security.

In cybersecurity, a high-risk appetite could mean taking calculated risks with specific technologies or initiatives and accepting potential vulnerabilities if the anticipated reward justifies the danger. Conversely, a business with a low-risk appetite, such as a government agency dealing with sensitive material, may opt for strict security procedures that reduce flexibility but minimize risk exposure.

Knowing an organization's risk appetite allows the security team to prioritize resources and efforts. For instance, if the digital wallet function was deemed unsafe without appropriate cybersecurity protocols, the team may focus on additional protective measures targeted to that particular product, balancing innovation with protection.

4. Vulnerability and Threat Scores

Definition: Vulnerability and threat scores measure the potential risk of security defects and the severity of recognized threats. These scores help teams prioritize issues based on possible effects.

Scenario: A manufacturing corporation is assessing the vulnerability of its Industrial Control Systems (ICS). The examination identifies several weaknesses; however, each has a different score. One vulnerability scores an 8.5 out of 10 (showing a high risk of exploitation and a severe impact), whereas another earns a 4.2 (indicating a lower likelihood and impact).

Using these scores, the security team can prioritize patching the high-score vulnerability first, ensuring significant gaps are filled. This technique is critical for resource allocation, allowing teams to focus attention on the most pressing threats.

Vulnerability and threat scoring systems, such as the Common Vulnerability Scoring System (CVSS), are widely used across sectors. They provide a standardized means of analyzing and conveying the severity of potential security vulnerabilities, allowing teams to design action plans that address the most crucial areas.

5. Exposure Factor (EF)

Definition: Exposure Factor (EF) is the percentage of an asset at risk if a given threat materializes. EF helps quantify the impact of a security incident on multiple assets, leading the organization's response and mitigation activities.

Scenario: Consider a telecoms corporation with a high-value customer database worth millions. In a data breach, the exposure factor might estimate that 70% of this database could be affected if proper measures aren't in place.

Understanding EF helps the team assess how much of their asset's value could be lost, leading to investment in backup systems or segmentation to mitigate possible losses. If they partition the database and reduce EF from 70% to 20%, even in a breach, they're better positioned to minimize financial effect.

EF is excellent for enterprises that rely substantially on high-value digital assets. By measuring EF, firms may estimate possible losses and take steps to protect vital assets more efficiently.

6. Single Loss Expectancy (SLE)

Definition: SLE calculates the expected financial loss from a single security incident. It's calculated by multiplying the asset's value by the exposure factor (SLE = Asset Value × EF).

Scenario: Let's assume a retail corporation with a valuable customer data asset valued at $500,000.

If the exposure factor for a data breach is assessed at 60%, the single loss expectancy (SLE) is $300,000. This value shows the possible financial impact of a breach.

Calculating SLE helps businesses understand the direct economic implications of various hazards. This knowledge is vital when determining the security measures to invest in. If the retail organization understands a breach may cost them $300,000, they may invest in better data protection techniques to lower the EF and minimize potential damage.

7. Annualized Loss Expectancy (ALE)

Definition: ALE calculates an organization's overall expected loss over a year. It's computed by multiplying SLE by the annual rate of occurrence (ARO) for a single incidence (ALE = SLE × ARO).

Scenario: A mid-sized corporation dealing with consumer payment data believes that the ARO of a data breach is 0.5 (or once every two years). With an SLE of $300,000 for each violation, the ALE becomes $150,000.

This statistic indicates to the firm what they anticipate losing annually due to data breaches. Knowing the ALE helps budget cybersecurity investments. If the ALE is high, the organization might prioritize more lavish security spending to mitigate potential losses. ALE gives a more holistic risk perspective, helping firms make long-term decisions about cybersecurity spending.

8. Security Incident and Event Management (SIEM) Metrics

Definition: SIEM metrics provide detailed data on security incidents and trends, from detection and response times to threat patterns. These indicators are critical for real-time threat monitoring and tracking progress toward cybersecurity targets.

Scenario: A tech corporation with a significant digital presence employs an SIEM system to monitor log data and discover suspicious patterns. The organization can spot threats in real-time by watching variables like failed login attempts, login locations, and file access patterns.

SIEM data also give insights into MTTD and MTTR, allowing teams to review and enhance their incident response operations. In this example, the IT business can observe if specific response processes shorten MTTR and try to repeat such protocols in future events.

SIEM metrics let enterprises benchmark their security performance over time, giving them a clear image of where they are and where changes are needed. This data-driven strategy provides proactive threat management, lowering the chance of costly occurrences.

9. Mean Time Between Failures (MTBF)

Definition: MTBF tracks the average time between system failures or security incidents, offering insight into system or process reliability.

Scenario: A financial services company relies on safe internet banking. It tracks MTBF to understand the frequency of system downtimes, such as disruptions in authentication services. If MTBF indicates events occurring too frequently, the firm can explore the root cause, possibly replacing obsolete security software or policies.

In cybersecurity, MTBF is essential for analyzing how effectively systems resist threats over time. Low MTBF levels reflect frequent difficulties that demand rapid attention, whereas high MTBF values indicate stable, well-functioning security systems.

Chapter 5

The Basics of Measurement Theory in Cybersecurity

At its foundation, measurement theory is all about the methodical way we assign numbers or values to things we want to investigate or regulate. In cybersecurity, the stakes are enormous, and knowing exactly what we're up against is essential. Effective measurement allows us to quantify threat levels, track improvements, and understand where our defenses need reinforcing. In reality, measurement theory is the backbone of every cybersecurity approach that strives to be proactive rather than reactive. Over the years, I've found that measuring creates clarity in working with teams. Without it, security strategies generally depend on gut reactions or assumptions—neither holds up well when an actual incident occurs.

By establishing our cybersecurity assessments using robust measurement methods, we move from "feeling secure" to quantitative certainty. This difference isn't just theoretical; it directly affects the organization's capacity to withstand and recover from attacks.

Types of Data in Cybersecurity

Regarding cybersecurity, we're dealing with two primary forms of data: qualitative and quantitative. Knowing when and how to use each type is vital for drawing correct conclusions and creating realistic goals.

1. Quantitative Data

Quantitative data is quantifiable and objective—think of measurements like the number of malware detections per month, the average time to patch vulnerabilities, or the proportion of systems that comply with security regulations. This quantitative data makes it excellent for analyzing trends over time or comparing one security control against another.

For instance, a corporation measuring the "mean time to detect" (MTTD) and "mean time to respond" (MTTR) can use quantitative data to assess if their incident response times are improving over months or quarters. The figures tell a straightforward story: a drop in these indicators means faster detection and reaction, whereas any increased trend signals possible areas for development.

2. Qualitative Data

While quantitative data offers us statistics, qualitative data adds context and depth. Qualitative data is descriptive and frequently subjective, capturing insights that are harder to evaluate mathematically but just as significant. Examples include employee input on cybersecurity training, customer worries about data security, or the level of user trust in corporate policies.

In cybersecurity, qualitative data helps us understand the "why" behind the numbers. For instance, if employees feel that phishing simulations are unrealistic or that security rules are excessively tight, such feedback can lead to training improvements or policy revisions.

When to Use Each Type of Data

Quantitative data helps track progress and discover patterns. It is excellent if you want to know how your response times have changed after deploying a new detection technology. Qualitative data, however, is essential when researching explanations behind particular trends.

If your incident response times are improving but staff morale is declining, qualitative insights might help uncover any friction points or pain regions that require attention.

Merging both data kinds produces a richer, more accurate picture. For instance, a team examining phishing risks might utilize quantitative data to measure the click-through rate on simulated phishing emails and qualitative data from employee comments to modify training materials, ensuring the numbers and the narrative align.

Common Misconceptions and Pitfalls in Cybersecurity Measurement

While necessary, measurement in cybersecurity comes with its fair share of misunderstandings.

Let's review some common misconceptions and the hazards they can lead to if left unchecked.

1. Misconception: "More Data Equals Better Security"

A prevalent notion is that collecting as much data as possible will necessarily increase security. In actuality, data overload can create more difficulties than it solves. When we're drowned in data, it gets tougher to distinguish what matters.

This happens when teams adopt a new SIEM system without explicitly outlining what they want to monitor. They end up with thousands of daily warnings, most of which are low-priority or false positives. The result? Critical concerns are lost in the hubbub.

The solution is to focus on quality over quantity. Define which metrics correspond with your quantifiable goals and collect data that serves those aims. By reducing down, you produce a manageable, actionable data collection that's easier to monitor and comprehend.

2. Misconception: "If It's Measured, It's Managed"

A widespread saying in business is that "if you can measure it, you can manage it." While measurement is vital, it's not enough on its own. I've dealt with teams that measure many metrics but fail to act on them. They know their MTTD, MTTR, and vulnerability scores—but without action plans, those metrics are just numbers on a screen.

Measuring metrics should always come with a plan of action. If MTTD isn't improving, consider probable fundamental causes— maybe it's a tool issue or a lack of training on incident detection. Actionable steps turn measurement into a catalyst for meaningful change.

3. Pitfall: Ignoring the Context of Metrics

Metrics don't exist in a vacuum; taking data out of context can lead to misinterpretation. For example, a sudden rise in login attempts can look like a brute-force assault, but context could reveal it was due to a system glitch or an update forcing all users to re-authenticate.

Misinterpreting measurements without context can lead to wasteful responses, wasting time and resources.

4. Pitfall: Over-Reliance on Benchmarking

While comparing against industry standards can be valuable, it's not necessarily appropriate in cybersecurity. Every organization has unique risks, resources, and threat profiles. Comparing your MTTD to that of a different industry might not be meaningful, as the obstacles and dangers can vary greatly. Instead, focus on internal benchmarks over time to see success within the specific context of your organization's risk picture.

5. Pitfall: Focusing Only on Lagging Indicators

Lagging indicators measure historical occurrences, like the number of incidents last month or the average downtime after an assault. While they help analyze historical performance, leading indicators, like patching speed or employee compliance rates with phishing training, can provide more proactive insights. Leading indicators help organizations stay ahead by addressing possible risks before they result in incidents.

Introduction to Key Metrics and KPIs for Cybersecurity

To establish a successful, proactive cybersecurity program, it's vital to track Key Performance Indicators (KPIs) that represent the organization's security goals and current threat landscape. Here are some of the most crucial KPIs for a well-rounded cybersecurity risk assessment:

1. Incident Response Time (IRT)

IRT quantifies the time it takes to detect a security incident and contain it. Shortening IRT helps lessen the possible harm and downtime associated with breaches. For example, suppose a team's IRT was five hours before implementing automated incident response tools and decreased to two hours thereafter. In that case, that reduction directly corresponds to a reduced probability of severe impact.

2. Patch Management Rate

This KPI records the percentage of detected vulnerabilities patched within a defined timeframe. Regular patching is crucial since attackers often exploit known vulnerabilities. An organization with a patch management target of addressing 90% of high-risk vulnerabilities within 48 hours might monitor this KPI to measure how successfully it accomplishes that goal.

3. False Positive Rate in Threat Detection

While detection systems are vital, they might overload security professionals if they generate too many false positives. The False Positive Rate (FPR) indicator tracks the proportion of security alarms that turn out to be harmless. A high FPR implies a need for better tuning or updating of detecting systems. For instance, if a financial company's FPR is 30%, decreasing it to 10% enhances the team's performance and guarantees serious concerns are addressed sooner.

4. User Awareness and Training Success Rate

Human error is one of the major reasons for security breaches. This KPI measures the success of cybersecurity training by tracking data like completion rates and simulated phishing click-through rates. For example, a corporation with a high phishing click-through rate might increase its training frequency and quantify effectiveness by reducing clicks over succeeding months.

5. Rate of Data Exfiltration Attempts

Data exfiltration attempts can flag potential insider threats or compromised systems. Monitoring this KPI helps firms spot questionable activity before it escalates. For example, a computer corporation might monitor how often sensitive files are viewed or transferred off the network, with spikes in this metric triggering an instant assessment by the security team.

6. Compliance Rate with Security Policies

Compliance with internal security policies, such as multifactor authentication (MFA) adoption or regular password updates, is a leading indicator of an organization's security posture. Tracking compliance rates helps identify departments or people wanting more training or support.

7. Rate of Successful Attacks vs. Attempted Attacks

This KPI compares the number of successful assaults to the number of attempted attacks, reflecting the effectiveness of an organization's defenses. For instance, a telecom corporation experiencing many attempted attacks with a low success rate could attribute its resilience to excellent threat detection and mitigation techniques.

8. Mean Time Between Failures (MTBF)

MTBF analyzes the average time between system failures or serious events, providing insight into the overall stability of the security infrastructure. A low MTBF could imply that key systems need updates or additional protective measures.

Chapter 3

Identifying and Defining Cybersecurity Risks

E ffective cybersecurity starts with understanding your opponent. Although cyber risks are complicated, they can be better controlled if we approach their definition and identification methodically. The fundamentals of risk identification, quantifiable risk definition, asset and threat inventory creation, and risk profile construction are covered in this chapter.

How to Identify Risks: Threat Modeling and Vulnerability Assessment

Two of our most effective tools for determining cybersecurity risks are vulnerability assessment and threat modeling. These procedures offer distinct yet complementary perspectives on our risk environment.

1. Threat Modeling

A proactive method for spotting possible risks and comprehending how they can affect your systems is threat modeling. Threat modeling enables us to foresee potential problems based on the assets we're attempting to safeguard and the strategies that attackers are likely to employ, rather than waiting for a security issue to arise. Because it allows us to think like an attacker, this method is extremely important in the field of cybersecurity.

Let's take the example of dealing with a financial services company. Potential risks including Distributed Denial of Service (DDoS) assaults, account takeovers, and data breaches may be discovered during a threat modeling session. The group would examine the company's infrastructure, examining the locations of sensitive data storage and possible points of access that hackers could use. We may implement measures to lessen the likelihood that these risks will materialize by anticipating and detecting them.

2. Vulnerability Assessment

Vulnerability assessments concentrate on finding vulnerabilities in our systems that could be exploited, whereas threat modeling focuses on detecting possible threats. In order to identify areas of risk, a vulnerability assessment methodically looks at an organization's hardware, software, network setups, and even personnel behaviors.

Using the financial services example once more, the vulnerability assessment may identify firewall configuration errors, out-of-date software on vital servers, or even a deficiency in multifactor authentication on employee accounts. Finding these vulnerabilities is the first step in preventing attackers from taking advantage of them. These evaluations are frequently carried out using tools like Nessus, Qualys, and Rapid7 InsightVM, which offer thorough findings that aid in setting patching and system hardening priorities.

By integrating threat modeling and vulnerability assessment, we may obtain a comprehensive understanding of potential threats to our systems and areas that require reinforcement.

Defining Risk in Measurable Terms

Making cybersecurity assessments actionable requires defining risk in quantifiable terms. In cybersecurity, risk is, in general, the likelihood that a threat would take advantage of a weakness to affect an asset. To quantify risk, we must divide it into three primary components: threats, vulnerabilities, and impact.

1. Probability of Threat Occurrence

Predictive analysis, industry trends, or historical data can all be used to determine the likelihood that a danger will materialize. We may give phishing threats a probability score, for instance, if a company has experienced five phishing attacks in the last 12 months. To maintain the accuracy of risk assessments in the face of emerging trends or threat patterns, this likelihood must be updated on a regular basis.

2. Likelihood of Vulnerability Exploitation**

Not every vulnerability has the same chance of being exploited. A vulnerability in a system that is only available internally, for example, might be less likely to be exploited than one in a web application that is accessible from the outside. Prioritizing vulnerabilities according to their accessibility to attackers is made easier by assigning likelihood scores.

3. Impact of Exploited Vulnerability

Lastly, impact refers to the possible harm resulting from a threat successfully taking advantage of a vulnerability. Financial, operational, reputational, and even legal repercussions are all possible. For instance, a data breach at a healthcare facility may result in legal action, regulatory penalties, and a decline in patient confidence. Calculating Single Loss Expectancy (SLE) or annualized loss expectancy (ALE) is a common step in impact measurement since it gives a specific number that can help with decision-making.

Example: If a business is concerned about ransomware, we could quantify the risk as follows:

The possibility of a ransomware assault

Probability: According to industry data, there is a 10% yearly chance of a ransomware attack in the sector.

Vulnerability: Insufficient network segmentation, which has a 50% chance of being exploited.

The expected financial impact in the event of a ransomware attack is $500,000.

We can generate a prioritized list of risks that directs the allocation of resources by decomposing risk in this manner.

How to Create an Inventory of Assets and Threats

Any cybersecurity program must include a thorough assessment of resources and threats. Risk assessments are insufficient if we don't know what we have and what can damage it. These are some methods for keeping track of these inventories.

1. Asset Inventory

Making an asset inventory entails listing everything in your surroundings that needs protection. These may consist of:

Examples of physical assets include computers, servers, network equipment, and other gear.

Examples of digital assets include databases, software programs, digital records, and intellectual property.

Workers, subcontractors, and other system users are considered human assets.

For instance, a financial services company may group its assets according to their level of importance: low-priority assets, such as publicly available material; medium-priority assets, such as marketing data; and high-priority assets, such as transaction databases.

Tool Spotlight: Many businesses automate asset discovery and classification using asset management systems like SolarWinds or Ivanti to keep inventory data current.

2. Threats Inventory

Making a threat inventory is the next step after you clearly understand your assets. This inventory lists and categorizes potential threats according to their type, likelihood, and potential impact. Typical dangers consist of:

External threats include ransomware, malware, DDoS attacks, phishing, and other attacks that originate outside the company.

Internal Threats: Insider threats from contractors or workers who abuse their position.

Environmental dangers include natural catastrophes, power outages, and other non-human hazards that could interfere with operations.

For instance, because of the operational and financial consequences of a disruption, a manufacturing company may rank threats to its production systems as a high priority. On the other hand, threats to employee communication channels may be less urgent but are still being watched.

3. Mapping Assets to Threats

To visualize which risks are the most significant to vital assets, we lastly map assets to pertinent threats. Usually, a threat modeling tool or a vulnerability management system is used to accomplish this.

For instance, mapping ransomware threats to an asset indicates the need for additional safeguards (such as data encryption or segmentation) if a financial institution determines that its client database is in great danger.

Case Study: Building a Risk Profile for a Mid-Sized Organization

Let's look at a real-world example of creating a risk profile for Tech Solutions Ltd., a mid-sized corporation that specializes in offering small businesses cloud-based data storage.

1. Asset and Threat Inventory

Tech Solutions begins by classifying its resources:

- Critical Assets: Cloud infrastructure, access control systems, and customer databases are examples of critical assets.

- Medium-Priority Assets: HR data and internal paperwork are considered medium-priority assets.

- Low-Priority Assets: Publicly accessible information and marketing materials.

Tech Solutions then develops a threat inventory.

- External Threats: Phishing, ransomware, and credential stuffing assaults are examples of external threats.

- Internal Threats: Unauthorized access by workers or contractors is one of the internal threats.

- Environmental Threats: Natural catastrophes and power outages that affect the data center are examples of environmental threats.

2. Vulnerability Assessment and Threat Modeling

After identifying the risks and assets, the Tech Solutions team conducts a threat modeling session. They concentrate on ransomware because, considering the company's reliance on cloud-based storage, it poses a high risk. According to the threat model, the absence of two-factor authentication (2FA) for administrators is one of the main vulnerabilities.

Additionally, they use Rapid7 InsightVM to assess vulnerability, which finds several unpatched vulnerabilities in externally accessible apps and obsolete software on several internal systems.

3. Defining Risk in Measurable Terms

The team's definition of ransomware risk is as follows, based on their findings:

- Threat: A ransomware assault that targets customer databases poses a threat.

- Probability: Based on industry data and the frequency of comparable accidents among competitors, the estimated probability is 8%.

Vulnerability: Administrator accounts do not have 2FA, which has a 60% chance of being exploited.

Impact: The estimated cost of a successful ransomware assault, including downtime, cleanup, and perhaps lost revenue, is $300,000.

4. Building the Risk Profile

Using all of this data, Tech Solutions creates a risk profile that lists the following:

Top Risks: insider threats, ransomware, and phishing attempts against staff members.

High-Priority Vulnerabilities: Outdated software on internal systems and administrator accounts without 2FA.

- Risk Mitigation Recommendations: Create a ransomware response plan, implement 2FA, patch software frequently, and do phishing scenarios for staff members.

A clear, actionable risk profile is the end outcome. Tech Solutions has a focused action plan to handle its most significant risks and knows where they are.

Chapter 4

Tools and Techniques for Accurate Data Collection

We require accurate, real-time data to comprehend what is occurring in our environment to quantify cybersecurity risk efficiently. Logs, surveys, and automated systems that offer insights into user behavior, system performance, and possible risks must be accessed to collect this data. In this chapter, we'll examine vital data-gathering strategies, the function of Security Information and Event Management (SIEM) systems, and ways to guarantee data quality. We'll also discuss a real-world example of how these tools might be configured in a business setting.

Overview of Data Collection Methods: Logs, Surveys, and Automated Tools

1. Logs

In cybersecurity, logs are the cornerstone of data collection. They serve as the company's digital trail, documenting everything from network activity and file modifications to system events and login attempts. Logs provide information about user behavior, system health, and anomalous activity that can point to danger when properly examined.

Each log type serves a unique purpose:

Access Logs: Monitor sensitive data access and user logins. Checking access logs can reveal unusual access patterns or illegal attempts.

Event logs: Keep track of system occurrences, including software upgrades, installations, and malfunctions. These logs are crucial for identifying anomalous activity and operational problems.

Application logs: Offer insight into how well apps operate and behave, which helps locate vulnerabilities or assaults at the application level.

While gathering and examining logs is crucial, handling them by hand may be very taxing. Systems and solutions that automate log gathering are useful here since they streamline the procedure and guarantee that no important information is missed.

2. Surveys and User Feedback

In cybersecurity, surveys are frequently disregarded, although they can provide valuable qualitative information, particularly when assessing the efficacy of security guidelines or training initiatives. Surveys can reveal information about employee behavior and attitudes toward cybersecurity, measure how well employees understand security procedures, and identify knowledge gaps.

A follow-up survey, for instance, might show whether staff members feel more comfortable identifying phishing attempts after implementing a new phishing awareness training. This input guarantees that the workforce is embracing cybersecurity activities and aids in improving training programs.

3. Automated Tools

Automated systems are revolutionary in terms of data collection since they provide real-time insights and lessen the workload for cybersecurity personnel. Network monitoring systems, Intrusion Detection Systems (IDS), and Endpoint Detection and Response (EDR) are examples of tools that continuously monitor network traffic and notify teams of any anomalous or suspicious activity.

For example, an EDR program placed on business laptops tracks file activity and detects anomalous patterns, like an unanticipated rise in network access or file copying. Automated technologies reduce the possibility of undetected risks by enabling organizations to take action on data as incidents occur.

How to Use SIEM and Other Systems to Achieve Real-Time Data

Systems for Security Information and Event Management (SIEM) are essential to contemporary cybersecurity. SIEMs compile information into a single dashboard from multiple sources, including logs, IDS, EDR tools, and more.

To expedite incident response, they prioritize and identify dangers based on their real-time analysis of this data.

How SIEM Work

A SIEM system gathers information from various sources, such as servers, firewalls, routers, and apps. Then, it normalizes and combines the data, using rules to find any trends or irregularities that might point to a security breach. Upon detecting a possible threat, the SIEM system creates warnings, ranking them according to their importance and seriousness.

Consider a mid-sized business where an extraordinary rise in unsuccessful login attempts from various IP addresses is detected by the SIEM instrument. By identifying this as a possible brute-force attack, the system notifies the security team, allowing them to look into it and take appropriate action before any unauthorized access takes place.

Benefits of Real-Time Data with SIEM

Immediate Threat discovery: SIEM systems can identify dangers as they arise thanks to real-time data, which shortens the period between discovery and reaction.

Centralized Monitoring:

SIEM creates a thorough picture of the organization's security posture by combining data from several sources.

Contextual Analysis:

SIEMs can give incidents context by correlating data from various sources. For instance, an SIEM might notice that a specific IP address has set off several alerts on multiple systems, suggesting a concerted attack.

Choosing the right SIEM Solution

The size of the company, industry standards, and available resources all play a role in selecting the best SIEM solution. Among the popular SIEM solutions in 2024 are ArcSight, IBM QRadar, and Splunk. Splunk is renowned for its robust data analytics, while QRadar is excellent at integrating threat information. Each of these solutions has unique qualities.

Cloud-based SIEMs, such as Microsoft Sentinel or Devo, provide scalability for small and mid-sized businesses without requiring on-premises infrastructure. Because these systems offer the same real-time monitoring as conventional SIEMs, enterprises with tight budgets can benefit from enhanced protection.

Data Quality and Ensuring Accuracy in Measurement:

Gathering data is one thing, but making sure it is accurate and of high quality is another. Poor data quality might result in inaccurate evaluations and conclusions. To guarantee data quality in cybersecurity measurements, follow these best practices.

a) Data accuracy

The process of verifying the accuracy of gathered data is known as data validation. This may consist of: Verifying that values fall within anticipated ranges is known as a range check.

Consistency checks: Confirming the logical consistency of connected facts. For instance, it could be worth looking into further if login times reveal that a user is accessing a system at 3 a.m. when they usually check in at 9 a.m.

Format checks: Making certain that information is gathered uniformly, particularly when combining information from several sources.

b). Normalization

When working with data that comes from several sources, normalization is very crucial. By standardizing data, it facilitates comparison and analysis. For example, log entries from various systems may have distinct formats for the timestamp. These formats can be normalized by an SIEM system, guaranteeing that all logs show consistent time entries, making correlation and analysis easier.

c). Reducing False Positives

Security teams may become overloaded with false positives, resulting in "alert fatigue." By fine-tuning detection rules in technologies like IDS and SIEM, teams can concentrate on real threats and reduce false positives. For example, the percentage of false alarms can be reduced by improving the detection criteria or providing contextual information if an intrusion detection system classifies normal network activity as worrisome.

d). Regular Audit

Frequent data quality audits assist in finding problems with data sources or collection techniques. For instance, a business may find that a setup problem is preventing some endpoints from reporting logs. Frequent checks increase the dependability of security metrics by ensuring that all systems are providing the SIEM with timely, reliable data.

How to Set Up Data Collection Processes in a Corporate Environment

Let's take a look at DataMart Inc., a mid-sized retail company that just launched its data-centric cybersecurity program, as a real-world example of how to set up data collecting for a corporate context.

1. Defining Data Collection Goals:

DataMart's security team starts by establishing clear objectives for data collection. One of their main goals is real-time detection of unwanted access attempts.

Keep an eye out for possible malware infestations on staff devices.

Make sure that only authorized workers can access sensitive consumer data.

2). Selecting Data Sources:

DataMart chooses the following data sources to achieve these objectives:

i). Their identity management system's access logs monitor who has access to private information and when.

ii). Network logs from routers and firewalls to track traffic patterns and search for possible intrusion attempts or DDoS attacks.

iii). Endpoint data from an EDR system to monitor for viruses and questionable file activity on staff devices.

3). Implementing a SIEM System:

DataMart chose Splunk as its SIEM solution due to its robust analytical capabilities and configurable dashboards. Splunk is set up to compile information from all chosen sources, giving security activity a centralized view.

4). Normalizing Data and Defining Alert Rules:

DataMart's IT staff normalizes the data within Splunk to guarantee consistency across logs from various sources. After that, they develop alert rules for particular occurrences, such as:

Several unsuccessful attempts to log in from the same IP address cause a high-priority alert for possible brute-force attacks.

A medium-priority alert for possible insider threats has been raised due to unusual file access on employee computers.

5). Ensuring Data Quality:

DataMart plans routine inspections to guarantee data quality. To reduce false positives, they perform weekly consistency checks, validate the data range for access logs, and frequently evaluate alert rules. By upholding data quality, DataMart guarantees that its SIEM warnings are pertinent and actionable.

6). Review and Continuous Improvement:

DataMart examines its data collection procedures three months later. They observe a rise in unsuccessful login attempts, which their SIEM correctly identified as brute-force efforts. DataMart monitors this pattern and strengthens its password policy, mandating multifactor authentication and stronger passwords for every employee. Thanks to this cycle of assessment and improvement, their data collection and security procedures are kept up to date with new threats.

Chapter 5

Quantitative Risk Analysis

Quantitative risk analysis expands cybersecurity evaluation beyond intuition, utilizing statistical methodologies and mathematical models to quantify and anticipate risk levels unlike qualitative assessment, which provides subjective risk categories (like "high" or "low"), quantitative analysis assigns numerical values to hazards, allowing for more exact, data-driven decisions. In cybersecurity, the risk is generally described as the chance of a threat exploiting a vulnerability and the possible impact if that threat is successful. To make these assessments relevant, we rely on statistical methods and probability, tools that help us quantify risk accurately and anticipate future accidents.

i). Probability is the possibility that a given event will happen. For instance, if a company's systems were targeted by malware twice last year, we may estimate the probability of a malware attack this year at 50%.

ii). Statistical Analysis helps us investigate patterns and trends throughout time. Using historical data and probability models, we may measure the possibility of events with identical features occurring in the future.

Statistical methodologies provide rigor to risk evaluations, giving a data-based foundation for cybersecurity decisions. Let's look at some critical quantitative models that apply these concepts to cybersecurity.

Standard Models: Monte Carlo Simulations, Bayesian Inference, and Loss Expectancy Calculations

1). Monte Carlo Simulations:

Monte Carlo simulations are vital for assessing risk through repeated random sampling. They are particularly effective when dealing with unknown or changeable inputs.

In cybersecurity, Monte Carlo simulations allow us to test a wide range of possible situations, giving a probability distribution that illustrates how often particular outcomes might occur.

Example: Imagine an organization wanting to estimate the possible financial impact of a ransomware attack. Utilizing a Monte Carlo simulation, they can input hypothetical ransom amounts, recovery times, and data restoration costs. The simulation executes thousands of events, providing a distribution of probable outcomes. If the most typical result suggests a possible loss of $250,000, the company can utilize this data point to steer its investment in defenses and insurance.

2). Bayesian Inference:

Bayesian inference is another statistically valuable method for updating risk evaluations when new information becomes available. Named for Reverend Thomas Bayes, it evaluates the likelihood of an event based on prior knowledge and new data.

Example: Suppose a cybersecurity team assesses a 20% chance of insider threats.

If, over time, they detect additional insider incidents, Bayesian inference allows them to alter that probability depending on the new data. This continuous updating makes Bayesian inference excellent for cybersecurity contexts because threat landscapes are continuously changing.

3). Loss Expectancy estimates:

ALE and SLE Loss expectancy estimates quantify the prospective financial impact of cyber catastrophes. There are two primary types of loss expectancy calculations:

Single Loss Expectancy (SLE):

Represents the estimated loss from a single incidence. SLE is calculated as: SLE=Asset Value×Exposure Factor (EF)SLE = \text{Asset Value} \times \text{Exposure Factor (EF)}SLE=Asset Value×Exposure Factor (EF)

4). Annualized Loss Expectancy (ALE): Represents the estimated annual loss, considering the chance of several events. ALE is calculated as: ALE=SLE×Annual Rate of Occurrence (ARO)ALE = SLE \times \text{Annual Rate of Occurrence (ARO)}ALE=SLE×Annual

Rate of Occurrence (ARO).

For example, if a financial organization values a sensitive database at $500,000, with an exposure ratio of 40%, the SLE for a breach is $200,000. If such a breach is predicted to occur twice a year (ARO = 2), the ALE becomes $400,000. This technique lets firms decide on security spending based on the possible annualized cost of events.

Building Quantitative Models for Cybersecurity Threats

Quantitative models allow us to turn theoretical concepts into actionable insights. By establishing a model, we create a framework that turns raw data into knowledge that informs decision-making.

1). Define Key Variables and Parameters Begin by determining the primary variables that impact risk. For a corporation concerned about phishing, these criteria might include:

Probability of Phishing Success: The possibility that a phishing attempt will deceive an employee.

Impact: The financial or operational effects of a successful phishing assault.

Response Time: The average time it takes to notice and respond to phishing occurrences.

2). Collect Relevant Data

Once variables are defined, gather historical and real-time data. If phishing is the focus, this can contain data from past phishing instances, staff training scores, and industry-wide statistics on phishing trends. The data should be as accurate and complete as feasible to maximize model reliability.

3). Create the Model

Using the data, construct a quantitative model that calculates the frequency and impact of phishing incidents. For instance, you could estimate the Annualized Loss Expectancy (ALE) by computing the expected financial loss per phishing episode and multiplying it by the anticipated frequency of attacks yearly.

4). Run Simulations and Scenarios

With your model in place, test it by running simulations and analyzing various scenarios.

For example, run a Monte Carlo simulation to anticipate the financial impact of phishing based on different attack frequencies or alter parameters to account for things like seasonal surges in phishing attempts (e.g., during tax season).

How to Calculate Risk Probability and Impact Using Real Data

Let's go over a real scenario to bring these concepts together. Imagine we're working with SecureData Solutions, a mid-sized IT company trying to quantify the risk associated with Distributed Denial of Service (DDoS) assaults. Here's how we'd approach the analysis:

1). Defining Variables and Collecting Data We start by identifying key variables:

Frequency of DDoS Attacks: SecureData's historical statistics show they've experienced two DDoS attacks per year for the past five years.

Impact: The typical impact of a DDoS attack, including lost productivity, cleanup costs, and potential customer churn, is assessed at $100,000.

With these variables, we have the basis for our calculations.

2). Calculating Single Loss Expectancy (SLE)
First, we calculate the Single Loss Expectancy for each attack. Since the average impact per event is $100,000 and the exposure factor is 1 (since each attack affects the entire system), our SLE is simply $100,000.

$$SLE = \text{Asset Value} \times \text{Exposure Factor}$$
$$SLE = 100,000 \times 1 = 100,000$$

3). Calculating Annualized Loss Expectancy (ALE)
Next, we calculate the ALE by multiplying the SLE by the frequency of expected attacks per year (ARO). With an ARO of 2, the ALE is:
$$ALE = SLE \times ARO$$
$$ALE = 100,000 \times 2 = 200,000$$

This calculation informs us that SecureData Solutions should anticipate an annual loss of

$200,000 from DDoS attacks if no further mitigations are employed.

4). Running a Monte Carlo Simulation for Variability:

To add nuance, we can run a Monte Carlo simulation. Instead of a fixed $100,000 per attack, we allow for a range of outcomes (say, $80,000 to $150,000) and run the calculation thousands of times to depict a realistic distribution of probable losses. The Monte Carlo statistics may reveal that, while $200,000 is a likely annual loss, there's a 10% possibility losses could exceed $300,000.

This insight helps Secure Data better comprehend worst-case scenarios and plan accordingly.

5). Using Bayesian Inference to Update the Model:

Finally, we employ Bayesian inference to update SecureData's risk model as new information becomes available. If DDoS attacks become more frequent industry-wide, Bayesian inference allows us to alter the ARO, delivering a dynamic, up-to-date risk estimate.

For example, if recent industry data predicts a 20% rise in DDoS attacks, SecureData can change its ARO from 2 to 2.4, boosting the ALE correspondingly. This adaptive strategy guarantees the company's risk model remains relevant as threat scenarios shift.

Chapter 6

How to Measure the Cost of Cybersecurity Incidents

Quantifying the cost of incidents is as vital in cybersecurity as developing protections. When a breach happens, it's not simply about recovering data or rebuilding systems; there are real, often large, financial losses involved. By identifying and analyzing these costs, organizations can make informed decisions about their cybersecurity budgets, allocate resources appropriately, and demonstrate the return on security investments.

Identifying Direct and Indirect Costs Associated with Security Breaches

To quantify the total cost of a cybersecurity incident, it's vital to consider both direct and indirect costs. Direct costs are usually transparent, such as the price of system repairs or legal fees.

Indirect costs, however, are typically more complicated to calculate but equally essential.

Direct Costs:

Incident Reaction and Forensic Analysis: One of the first expenses after a breach is the early reaction. This includes paying for incident response teams and forensic experts who examine the scope and origin of the breach. For example, a forensic analysis can cost tens of thousands of dollars, especially if the breach is extensive.

- System Recovery and Repairs:

The next stage is repairing or replacing damaged systems after controlling the breach. This could require reconfiguring networks, restoring data from backups, or, in certain situations, replacing hardware.

- Legal and Regulatory Fines:

Many sectors are subject to severe data privacy restrictions. If client data is compromised, firms may face substantial fines. In 2024, GDPR fines for data breaches can reach up to €20 million or 4% of annual global turnover—whichever is higher.

- Notification and Credit Monitoring:

In circumstances where personal data is involved, firms often need to contact affected customers, which involves costs linked to communication, call center support, and credit monitoring services.

Indirect Costs:
Reputational Damage:
A cyber event can harm a brand's image, causing loss of customers and lower trust. This is particularly costly for consumer-facing companies like retail or finance, where customer loyalty is crucial.

- Loss of Business Opportunities:
Downtime during and after a breach can lead to lost sales, disrupted services, or missed business opportunities. For example, if a retailer's e-commerce site drops, it loses direct sales and prospective future customers.

- Increased Insurance Premiums:
Many organizations carry cyber insurance, which can help alleviate some of the direct expenses of a breach. However, insurance premiums often climb after a claim, adding to long-term expenditures.

Using Historical Data to Predict Future Costs

Predicting the financial impact of potential cybersecurity events is challenging but doable by exploiting historical data. Many businesses collect information on prior incidences to determine cost patterns and trends, helping forecast future spending.

1). Cost Analysis of Past Incidents
Organizations might look at historical data to estimate likely expenses. For instance, if a financial services organization faced three phishing assaults last year with an average cost of $50,000 per incident, it could assume similar expenditures in the future year unless preventative measures are enhanced. Analyzing prior occurrences helps the organization forecast future spending and designate an adequate cybersecurity and incident response budget.

2). Benchmarking Against Industry Standards
Using industry data to benchmark expenses is another successful strategy. Many firms use the Ponemon Institute's Cost of a Data Breach Report, which estimates average expenses based on industry, breach size, and response time. In 2024, the average data breach cost for U.S.-based companies was around $4.45 million. By comparing internal costs with industry benchmarks,

companies can receive insight into whether their incident costs are above or below the average and take action to reduce them.

3). Adjusting Costs for Inflation and Changing Threats
Historical data alone isn't enough—cost estimates should account for inflation and the dynamic threat situation. With ransomware instances and phishing assaults increasing regularly, the possibility and effect of breaches are higher. Organizations should revise their estimations annually to reflect these developments.

Calculating ROI for Cybersecurity Investments

One of the most compelling approaches to justify cybersecurity spending is analyzing the Return on Investment (ROI). This technique demonstrates how security expenditures lower incident costs over time, demonstrating value beyond compliance or peace of mind.

1). Determine the Expected Savings
Expected savings from cybersecurity expenditures are calculated by comparing the predicted event costs with and without the investment. For instance, if a retail organization believes it will cut phishing

occurrences by 30% using sophisticated email filtering, the cost savings can be determined by assuming the average cost per phishing attack and the predicted reduction in incidents.

2). Calculate the Cost of the Investment
The cost of the investment comprises the upfront cost of purchasing tools or training programs and maintenance and operating expenses over time. For example, if the retail company invests $100,000 on a new security gadget with a monthly maintenance price of $10,000, the total cost over three years would be $130,000.

3). Apply the ROI Formula
The ROI formula is: ROI=Expected Savings - Cost of Investmen tCost of Investment×100\text{ROI} = \frac{\text{Expected Savings - Cost of Investment}}{\text{Cost of Investment}} \times 100ROI=Cost of Investment Expected Savings - Cost of Investment×100

Using the retail company example, if the tool is predicted to save $300,000 in prevented phishing charges over three years, the ROI would be:
ROI=300,000−130,000130,000×100=130. 8%\text{ROI}=\frac{300,000 -

130,000}{130,000} \times 100 = 130.8\%ROI=130,000300,000−130,000 ×100=130.8%

A positive ROI of 130.8% illustrates that the investment in the security solution will pay for itself and provide considerable savings over three years, making it a financially viable decision.

Case Study: Estimating Costs in a Retail Organization After a Cyber Breach
To demonstrate these concepts in action, let's examine a case study using RetailConnect, a mid-sized retail company that suffered a data breach that affected its e-commerce platform.

1). Incident Overview
RetailConnect faced a cyber compromise during the holiday season, compromising consumer financial credentials and resulting in a week-long outage on their e-commerce platform. The hack was tracked back to a phishing email targeting an employee in the IT department, who unintentionally provided credentials that allowed attackers access to essential systems.

2). Direct Costs Incident Response and System Repairs: RetailConnect spent $80,000 on incident response teams and system repairs, including rearranging its servers and updating security standards.

Legal Fees and Regulatory Fines: Due to data privacy rules, RetailConnect was fined $50,000 by regulatory authorities and incurred an extra $20,000 in legal fees.

Notification and Credit Monitoring:
The corporation paid $30,000 to notify affected clients and provide a year of credit monitoring services. Total Direct Costs: $180,000.

3). Indirect Costs Reputational Damage: RetailConnect saw a 15% decline in online sales during the next quarter, resulting in an estimated revenue loss of $120,000. The loss was primarily attributable to unfavorable media coverage and customer mistrust following the hack.

Increased Cyber Insurance Premium: Following the incident, the company's cyber insurance rates climbed by 25%, adding an extra $10,000 yearly to its operating expenses.

Loss of Business Opportunities: The breach forced RetailConnect to postpone the launch of a new loyalty program, which was anticipated to earn an additional $50,000 in sales for the quarter. Total Indirect Costs: $180,000.

Calculating Total Cost

By combining direct and indirect costs, RetailConnect assessed the entire financial impact of the breach:

$$\text{Total Cost} = \text{Direct Costs} + \text{Indirect Costs} = 180,000 + 180,000 = 360,000$$

Predicting Future Costs

RetailConnect investigated the incident to calculate the likely expenses of similar breaches in the future. Using historical data, they predicted that phishing attempts had a 15% likelihood of reoccurring annually, with comparable cost implications. By investing in advanced email filtering and personnel training, RetailConnect projected it could lower this risk by at least 50%.

ROI of Cybersecurity Investment

RetailConnect agreed to invest in a $60,000 phishing protection program, including email filtering, employee training, and simulated phishing tests. Based on predicted

savings from lower incident costs, the ROI was computed as follows:
Expected
Savings=360,000×50%=180,000\text{Exp ected Savings} = 360,000 \times 50\% = 180,000Expected
Savings=360,000×50%=180,000
ROI=180,000−60,00060,000×100=200%\ text{ROI} = \frac{180,000 - 60,000}{60,000} \times 100 = 200\%ROI=60,000180,000−60,000 ×100=200%

This 200% ROI highlighted the financial benefit of the investment, indicating that it would not only cover its costs but also result in significant long-term savings.

Chapter 7

Risk Communication and Visualization

T he most potent cybersecurity findings are only practical if presented correctly and strategically. Communicating risk isn't just about delivering data; it's about explaining what it means to decision-makers, ensuring they understand the relevance and can act on it. In this chapter, we'll discuss the necessity of conveying risk measurements, primary visualization tools, and strategies for customizing communication to diverse audiences. By the end, we'll also walk through an example of designing a cybersecurity risk assessment that connects with executives.

The Importance of Communicating Risk Metrics to Stakeholders:

For cybersecurity to be a priority across a business, it has to be understood at all levels. This is where communication becomes crucial. Effective risk communication helps stakeholders—from technical teams to executives—understand the security picture, the possible effects of threats, and the reasons for cybersecurity investments.

1). Building Support for Cybersecurity Initiatives:

When risk measurements are conveyed correctly, they provide a foundation of support for cybersecurity activities. For instance, if the CFO knows the potential financial consequence of a phishing attack, they're more likely to endorse an investment in advanced phishing training. Communicating measures like Annualized Loss Expectancy (ALE) in terms of future cost reductions can create a strong case for proactive expenditure, helping to secure essential resources.

2). Enhancing Decision-Making:
Clear risk communication helps leaders make informed decisions, influencing how they allocate resources, respond to incidents, and prioritize security efforts.

Presenting indicators such as Mean Time to Detect (MTTD) or compliance rates gives executives a clear view of present risks and areas that require improvement, helping them set realistic goals and expectations.

3). Fostering a Risk-Aware Culture:
Risk communication isn't just for CEOs; it's also vital for developing a culture of cybersecurity awareness across the organization. Metrics like phishing susceptibility rates or endpoint compliance percentages assist employees in comprehending the impact of their activities. This data can help reinforce training and foster a shared commitment to cybersecurity.

Visualization Techniques: Dashboards, Heat Maps, and Risk Matrices

Visualization is an excellent approach to communicating cybersecurity metrics. It turns complex data into digestible insights, helping stakeholders appreciate the relevance of risk measurements at a look.

1). Dashboards
Dashboards provide a real-time view of cybersecurity indicators and trends. A well-designed dashboard is often the first thing a stakeholder sees when analyzing an

organization's security posture. It can include indicators like incident frequency, patching progress, and threat detection times, giving an instant overview of the organization's position.

Example: A dashboard for a retail firm might display the number of blocked malware attempts, phishing detection rates, and open vulnerabilities. By personalizing each widget, dashboards can deliver tailored insights for specific teams or leaders, highlighting metrics corresponding to each group's priorities.

2). Heat Maps
Heat maps are an effective tool for showing the likelihood and impact of certain risks visually. By employing color gradients, heat maps make it easy to identify high-risk locations that require quick action.

Example: A heat map for a healthcare business might display high-risk categories such as unauthorized access and ransomware in darker hues. This color-coding provides a rapid snapshot of the locations most susceptible, letting teams prioritize resources based on risk levels.

3). Risk Matrices

Risk matrices are a typical tool for visualizing the probability and potential impact of risks. By putting these two dimensions on a grid, risk matrices let stakeholders evaluate risks in an organized fashion.

Example: For a financial services organization, a risk matrix might indicate high-probability, high-impact risks such as data breaches in the upper right corner, while low-probability, low-impact risks like minor system faults appear in the lower left. This framework supports determining priorities, making it obvious where the organization should spend its efforts.

How to Tailor Communication for Non-Technical and Executive Audiences:

While technical teams work with risk data daily, non-technical stakeholders and executives frequently need a different approach. Tailoring risk communication to these audiences is critical for effective decision-making and buy-in.

1). Simplify the Terminology

Avoid jargon and focus on plain, succinct language. For example, rather than describing a threat using technical jargon like "DDoS mitigation latency," use "the time it takes to block an online attack." Reducing language makes the message accessible to all stakeholders, independent of technical background.

2). Highlight the Business Impact
Non-technical stakeholders are more interested in the business ramifications than the technical aspects. Instead of reporting the probability of a danger, explain its potential consequence in terms of financial loss, operational interruption, or reputational damage. This makes the risk accessible and substantial to executives who are primarily focused on the bottom line.

Example: When presenting the risk of a phishing attack, frame it in terms of the possible cost of lost productivity or the resources needed to recover from an incident. This makes it easier for non-technical audiences to appreciate the necessity for preventive measures.

3). Use Comparisons and Benchmarks
Putting measurements in context with industry benchmarks or prior performance might help non-technical audiences grasp their relevance. For instance, if the organization's incident response time is

20% slower than the industry average, stakeholders will be more likely to recognize the need for improvement.

Example: A bank may compare its phishing detection rate to the industry average to demonstrate that its current rate is either strong or needs improvement. Comparisons like this add context, converting raw data into valuable insights.

4). Focus on Visual Summaries
Visuals like charts, graphs, and summary boxes help deliver the message swiftly. Executives frequently don't have the time to look into extensive reports, so a well-placed bar graph demonstrating month-to-month gains or a pie chart illustrating compliance rates can convey vital information effectively.

Practical Example: Designing an Executive-Friendly Cybersecurity Risk Report:

Let's build a cybersecurity risk report targeted at an executive audience. SecureBank, a regional financial institution, seeks to brief its board on cybersecurity threats and recent measures. Here's how they might design their report for maximum impact.

1). Executive Summary
Start with a one-page executive summary that emphasizes crucial themes. This section should include:
Top Three Risks: Summarize the organization's most critical risks, such as phishing, insider threats, and ransomware, and their potential impact.

2). Risk Reduction Achievements: Briefly describe recent gains, like a 20% reduction in phishing occurrences after establishing a new awareness campaign.

Key measures: Include two or three essential measures, such as MTTD and MTTR, to illustrate progress in detection and reaction times.

3). Dashboard View
The first visual in the report is a dashboard picture summarizing key metrics:
Incidents by Category: A bar chart illustrating the number of occurrences by kind (e.g., phishing, malware, unauthorized access) over the past quarter.

Response Times: A line graph illustrating changes in response times month over month, emphasizing any noticeable drops after specific initiatives.

Vulnerability Status: A pie chart indicating the percentage of critical, high, medium, and low vulnerabilities discovered, highlighting progress in patching high-risk regions.

4). Risk Heat Map
Next, SecureBank features a heat map illustrating current cybersecurity risks:
High-probability, high-impact hazards (e.g., phishing and ransomware) are underlined in red, drawing rapid attention.

Medium-probability, high-impact hazards (e.g., DDoS attacks) appear in orange, demonstrating they are still important but less urgent.

Lower-priority hazards, such as low-impact software faults, are in lighter shades.

The heat map provides a snapshot of the bank's most critical vulnerabilities, helping the board identify priorities.

5). Business Impact Analysis
SecureBank includes a business effect study component that quantifies prospective costs:

Phishing: Estimated annual cost based on past instances, including lost productivity, customer attrition, and remedial charges.

Insider Threats: Potential legal and reputational implications if sensitive consumer data is compromised.

Ransomware: Expected expenditures if recovery takes more than two days, depending on existing response capabilities.

This section converts technical hazards into commercial terms by quantifying the financial effect of each risk, making them more relevant to the board.

6). Actionable Recommendations
The final section contains concrete ideas for increasing cybersecurity posture:
Investment in AI-Driven Detection Tools: Highlight predicted increases in MTTD and phishing detection accuracy, portrayed as a high-ROI investment.

Additional Employee Training: Justify training with metrics indicating reduced incidents in departments that received improved training.

Upgrading Endpoint Security: Emphasize the necessity of endpoint protection by exhibiting current instances involving personal devices.

By tying each recommendation to particular indicators, SecureBank makes it easy for executives to evaluate how proposed measures match risk reduction targets.

Chapter 8

Continuous Monitoring and Improvement

Cybersecurity isn't static; it requires adaptability to a shifting threat scenario. As new vulnerabilities develop and attackers become more sophisticated, enterprises must keep their defenses nimble and responsive. Continuous monitoring and improvement shift cybersecurity from reactive to proactive and resilient, enabling firms to identify hazards in real time, respond rapidly, and modify their plans. In this chapter, we'll discuss the setup for continuous risk assessment, the role of automation, and techniques for adjusting to change, along with a practical example of a constant improvement cycle.

Setting Up Systems for Continuous Risk Assessment and Response:

Continuous monitoring entails more than just installing a security application; it demands a systematic method that includes real-time data collecting, analysis, and reaction. Setting up an effective continuous monitoring system begins with defining important risk indicators, picking acceptable technologies, and developing explicit guidelines for action.

1. Defining Key Risk Indicators (KRIs)

KRIs are measurable measures highlighting potential security threats, allowing teams to keep a pulse on their surroundings. Common KRIs include:

- Anomalous Login Attempts: Unusual patterns in login attempts may suggest brute-force assaults or unauthorized access.

- Data Exfiltration Rates: An increase in data transfers from a sensitive database can signal probable data theft.

- Phishing Success Rates: Monitoring click-through rates on phishing simulations helps analyze the organization's vulnerability to social engineering.

By putting up alerts for certain KRIs, security personnel are notified as soon as unexpected activity occurs, allowing them to intervene before an incident escalates.

2. Establishing a Framework for Response

When setting up continuous monitoring, a defined incident response strategy is necessary. Organizations like NIST and ISO provide established guidelines, but they need to be customized to each organization's specific situation. Define roles and duties for each team member, including who reviews alerts, initiates the incident response process, and engages with stakeholders.

- Example: A healthcare organization might have a dedicated security team that monitors monitoring but relies on a cross-departmental team to respond to specific threats, such as ransomware. Clear roles and protocols streamline the response process, saving downtime and maintaining compliance with requirements like HIPAA.

3. Continuous Risk Assessment through Threat Hunting

Beyond automatic monitoring, threat hunting is a proactive strategy for finding hidden threats. Threat hunting requires personally researching patterns, abnormalities, and questionable activities that automated methods could ignore. By incorporating threat hunting into continuous monitoring, businesses can find advanced threats, such as zero-day vulnerabilities or insider threats, that defy traditional protections.

Using Automated Tools for Real-Time Data Collection and Threat Monitoring

Automation is the cornerstone of continuous monitoring. With automated technologies, companies can collect and analyze data in real-time, decreasing the need for manual inspections and accelerating response times.

1. Security Information and Event Management (SIEM) Systems

SIEM systems are crucial to automated monitoring. They combine data from many sources—such as firewalls, intrusion detection systems (IDS), and endpoint protection tools—and analyze it for potential threats. SIEMs like Splunk, IBM QRadar, and

Microsoft Sentinel enable real-time threat detection and configurable warnings.

- Example: A mid-sized store using IBM QRadar configures the SIEM to monitor credit card data access attempts in its databases. The system raises an alert whenever an unexpected access pattern is observed, prompting an immediate inquiry. This approach lets the business avoid data breaches, protecting critical consumer information.

2. Endpoint Detection and Response (EDR)

EDR technologies like CrowdStrike, SentinelOne, and Carbon Black provide deep insights into endpoint activity, such as file downloads, process execution, and user behavior. These technologies can detect anomalies and flag activities indicative of malware or illegal access attempts.

- Example: An EDR system distributed across all business laptops can identify when an employee mistakenly downloads a harmful attachment. The EDR program automatically isolates the afflicted device, preventing the infection from spreading further across the network.

3. Network Traffic Analysis Tools

Network traffic analysis (NTA) technologies analyze data flows throughout the network, helping detect odd traffic patterns that may suggest a cyber assault. NTA products like Darktrace, ExtraHop, and Corelight use machine-learning algorithms to discern regular traffic from suspicious actions.

- Example: A financial institution may utilize Darktrace to monitor traffic trends. If the program identifies an abnormal rise in data transfers from a particular department, it quickly raises the alarm, allowing the security team to investigate and intervene if necessary.

Adapting to Changes: Keeping Measurement Relevant as Threats Evolve

Risk measurement approaches must develop in response as cyber threats become increasingly sophisticated. This includes remaining educated about new attack vectors, periodically reassessing risk indicators, and making thoughtful adjustments to security policies.

1. Regular Review and Adjustment of KRIs

KRIs are crucial for continuous monitoring, but they must be routinely reviewed. For example, in 2024, ransomware techniques have changed from primarily encrypting files to exfiltrating data and threatening to release it if ransomware isn't paid. Organizations should update KRIs to reflect these new strategies, tracking encryption attempts and data exfiltration rates.

2. Adopting New Technologies and Techniques

Emerging technologies like artificial intelligence (AI) and machine learning (ML) are revolutionizing cybersecurity. By adopting AI-powered solutions, firms may automate threat detection and even identify dangers before they arise.

- Example: An AI-driven tool that examines historical attack trends could forecast when and how specific departments might be targeted. For instance, if phishing assaults tend to surge in the HR department around tax season, AI can inform the team to prepare countermeasures in advance, decreasing risk.

3. Engaging in Continuous Learning and Threat Intelligence Sharing

Staying informed is crucial to sustaining an adaptive security approach. Cybersecurity staff should frequently attend training, analyze industry studies, and participate in threat intelligence-sharing platforms. Platforms like ISAC (Information Sharing and Analysis Centers) give immediate intelligence on developing risks, which enterprises can integrate into their continuous monitoring framework.

- Example: If a threat-sharing platform indicates a spike in credential-stuffing attacks targeting retail, an e-commerce company might tighten password rules and adopt two-factor authentication to fight against this attack preemptively.

Case Study: Implementing a Continuous Improvement Cycle in Cybersecurity

To illustrate the constant monitoring and improvement process, let's look at SecureHealth, a healthcare firm dedicated to preserving patient data and ensuring compliance with HIPAA.

1. Setting Up Initial Monitoring Systems

SecureHealth begins by adopting an SIEM system, Splunk, to collect and analyze data from essential systems, such as electronic health records (EHR) and network firewalls. They define KRIs as including:

- Unusual Data Access Patterns: Monitoring patient record access rates to detect probable insider threats.

- Data Transfer Volumes: Setting thresholds for data exfiltration to identify potential breaches.

- Phishing Incident Rate: Tracking click-through rates on simulated phishing emails to measure staff knowledge.

2. Integrating Automated Tools for Real-Time Monitoring

In addition to SIEM, SecureHealth delivers an EDR solution across all employee workstations and laptops. This EDR program alerts questionable endpoint activity, such as unexpected file downloads or network connections, and isolates compromised machines if malware is found.

They include Darktrace's NTA technology for network security, which employs machine learning to identify traffic irregularities. These systems provide round-the-clock protection, ensuring the team receives real-time notifications on potential security occurrences.

3. Implementing a Continuous Improvement Cycle

With monitoring in place, SecureHealth adopts a continuous improvement cycle as follows:

- Quarterly Review of KRIs and Metrics: SecureHealth examines its KRIs and performance measures every quarter. Of one assessment, they find a persistent trend of phishing incidents affecting the HR department. As a reaction, they offer more targeted training sessions for HR workers and install a more robust email filtering technology.

- Post-Incident Analysis and Updates: SecureHealth conducts a complete analysis after every event. For example, during a recent ransomware attempt, the team uncovered holes in endpoint defenses. This led to modifying the EDR solution to handle a broader range of file types and creating a more robust access control policy for administrators.

- Benchmarking and Adjustments:
SecureHealth benchmarks its security performance to industry standards. They notice that their MTTR (Mean Time to Respond) is slightly above average. By automating specific response duties and optimizing incident response workflows, they cut MTTR by 15% over the next quarter.

4. Adapting to New Threats with Threat Intelligence

SecureHealth maintains an updated list of emerging risks with an ISAC for the healthcare sector. When the ISAC reports increased data extortion tactics, SecureHealth takes preemptive precautions, including encrypting important files at rest and creating a "least privilege" access policy. This adaptation mitigates the possibility of extortion and increases the overall security posture.

5. Reporting to Stakeholders
Finally, SecureHealth delivers monthly reports to its leadership team, highlighting

incident frequency, reaction times, and improvements made over the preceding period. By frequently reporting accomplishments, the team generates support for ongoing investments in cybersecurity.

These reports showcase the visible benefit of continuous monitoring, showing decreases in incidents and reaction times and indicating that security investments deliver measurable improvements.

Chapter 9

Case Studies and Best Practices In Cybersecurity

Healthcare: Protecting Patient Data with Continuous Monitoring The healthcare industry has unique issues due to tight compliance regulations like HIPAA and the necessity to preserve sensitive patient data. HealthFirst Network, a mid-sized hospital system, faced frequent phishing incidents targeting staff and triggering data breaches. By adopting continuous monitoring using endpoint detection and response (EDR) technologies, HealthFirst was able to trace phishing activities and monitor staff behavior. After rolling out a robust data-measuring methodology, HealthFirst witnessed a 40% reduction in successful phishing events within the first year. Additionally, the firm employed Key Performance Indicators (KPIs) to measure and alter training programs, leading to better security awareness across departments.

HealthFirst's experience illustrates how data-driven continuous monitoring, paired with targeted employee training, can significantly improve cybersecurity in the healthcare sector, where patient trust and regulatory compliance are crucial.

Government: Standardizing Risk Measurement with NIST Framework

Government agencies confront varied cybersecurity concerns due to the volume of sensitive information they handle. CityGov Solutions, a local government organization, embraced the NIST Cybersecurity Framework to implement consistent security policies across its numerous divisions. The agency measured compliance rates, patch management timelines, and incident reaction times as part of its risk assessment process.

By employing measurement to unify its security efforts, CityGov improved compliance with internal regulations by 25% and decreased its patching window from 60 to 30 days.

The agency also conducted quarterly risk assessments, enabling it to identify and resolve problems proactively. CityGov's approach shows the value of combining data-driven measurement with a cybersecurity framework, resulting in greater accountability and a more resilient security posture across the company.

Lessons Learned from Measurement Failures and How to Avoid Them

Success stories are exciting, but there's also a lot to learn from examples of measuring attempts that failed. Organizations can avoid typical errors by recognizing these failures and establishing a more rigorous measuring plan.

Lesson 1: Avoiding Overcomplicated Metrics in Retail

RetailNow Corp, a national retailer, invested extensively in a sophisticated cybersecurity measurement system. However, the indicators they tracked were highly complex, making it impossible for teams to analyze the data. Critical insights became lost, leading to delayed reactions to cyber disasters.

Lesson: Simplify metrics to ensure clarity. Choose important KPIs that reflect the organization's primary security goals and are straightforward to communicate to all stakeholders. Instead of collecting thousands of data, RetailNow should have concentrated on several KPIs, such as incident response times and phishing success rates, which would have provided helpful information without overwhelming the team.

Lesson 2: Ignoring Data Quality in Manufacturing

ManufactureSecure Inc., a worldwide manufacturing corporation, employed data-driven measurement to track vulnerabilities and patch management. However, they failed to maintain data quality, and improper logging techniques led to uneven outcomes. In one instance, they overlooked a significant vulnerability owing to data inconsistencies, resulting in an expensive ransomware assault.

Lesson: Prioritize data quality to achieve reliable measurements. Conduct regular audits, validate data sources, and standardize data collection processes to prevent errors.

A dedication to data integrity enables more precise risk assessments and eliminates potentially costly oversights, especially in areas where tiny oversights can interrupt production and affect profitability.

Lesson 3: Failure to Adapt in Higher Education
UniProtect Network, a higher education institution, tracked its cybersecurity metrics well for numerous years. However, UniProtect failed to update its Key Risk Indicators and analytics correctly as threats developed. This static approach meant emerging dangers, including credential stuffing and cloud-based attacks, went unnoticed, resulting in breaches.

Lesson: Regularly examine and update measurements to respond to evolving risks. Cybersecurity is a dynamic field, and measurement must evolve with it. By frequently reassessing KRIs, UniProtect might have better linked its security measurements with the current threat landscape, protecting both its data and its students.

How to Manage Cybersecurity Risk
Establish Clear, Relevant KPIs, and KRIs: KPIs and KRIs are crucial to good

assessment. Begin by setting goals that match your organization's specific risk profile. Focus on a limited set of data, such as phishing success rates, time to patch vulnerabilities, and compliance rates with security standards, to deliver clear, actionable insights without overloading the team.

- Automate Wherever Possible:

Cyber threats evolve swiftly, and real-time monitoring is essential for staying ahead. Automated technologies, like SIEM and EDR systems, are crucial for continuous monitoring, as they collect and analyze data at a scale that manual methods simply can't match. Automation eliminates human error, boosts efficiency, and ensures that critical dangers are caught as they happen.

- Foster a Risk-Aware Culture Across the Organization:

Cybersecurity isn't simply the duty of the IT department; it's a company-wide commitment. Regular training sessions, simulated phishing exercises, and accessible security reporting create a risk-aware culture that minimizes human weaknesses. Measure employee involvement in training programs and follow progress over time to ensure that awareness activities make a visible difference.

- Regularly Audit and Refine Metrics:
Audits ensure that your data and metrics remain accurate and relevant. Perform quarterly or biannual audits to evaluate data integrity, review KRIs, and assess the effectiveness of current security policies. Update measurements to reflect new threats, develop technology, and increase industry norms.

- Prioritize Communication and Stakeholder Buy-In:
Effective cybersecurity requires stakeholders' buy-in. Tailor communication techniques to varied audiences—use graphic dashboards for CEOs and detailed reports for technical teams. Showcasing the financial benefit of cybersecurity initiatives, such as the ROI of a new phishing prevention program, creates support for ongoing investments.

Appendices:

Appendix A: Glossary of Key Terms

Mean Time to Detect (MTTD): The average time it takes to identify a cybersecurity incident.

Mean Time to Respond (MTTR): The average time it takes to contain and remedy an event following detection.

Key Risk Indicator (KRI): A statistic used to signal a potential cybersecurity danger.

Key Performance Indicator (KPI): A metric used to quantify the effectiveness of cybersecurity processes and controls.

Appendix B: Cybersecurity Tools and Resources

SIEM Solutions: IBM QRadar, Splunk, Microsoft Sentinel

EDR Tools: CrowdStrike, SentinelOne, Carbon Black

Training Platforms: KnowBe4, Infosec IQ, PhishMe Threat Intelligence Platforms: ISAC, MISP, Anomali

Appendix C: Sample Risk Assessment Templates

Risk Assessment form: A standard form for assessing and categorizing cybersecurity threats.

Incident Response Checklist: A step-by-step checklist for organizing and recording response actions following an incident.

Metrics Dashboard Layout: A flexible layout for establishing a cybersecurity dashboard containing placeholders for critical KPIs and KRIs.

www.ingramcontent.com/pod-product-compliance
Lightning Source LLC
LaVergne TN
LVHW051652050326
832903LV00032B/3769